CREATIVE
BEAD JEWELLERY

CREATIVE
BEAD JEWELLERY

A practical guide to forty inspirational

designs with beads

Sara Withers

APPLE

A QUINTET BOOK

Published by The Apple Press
6 Blundell Street
London N7 9BH

ISBN 1-85076-619-3

This book was designed and produced by
Quintet Publishing Limited
6 Blundell Street
London N7 9BH

CREATIVE DIRECTOR: *Richard Dewing*
DESIGNER: *Simon Balley*
PROJECT EDITOR: *Diana Steedman*
EDITOR: *Karin Fancett*
PHOTOGRAPHER: *Paul Forrester*

Typeset in Great Britain by
Central Southern Typesetters, Eastbourne
Manufactured by Regent Publishing Services Ltd, Hong Kong
Printed by Leefung-Asco Printers Ltd, China

introduction

~

Over the last few years, many of us appear to have gone a little "bead crazy." You can now buy T-shirts emblazoned with the words "Bead Addict," or fabrics that are patterned with bead designs. There are many retail, mail-order, and wholesale suppliers of beads, a British company that specializes in bead parties for children, and any number of bead societies, fairs, and symposiums. Perhaps the idea that

introd

Manhattan was bought for a handful of beads is a myth – but the bead-trading tradition is flourishing in America, and in other parts of the world. Britain has a large number of beadworkers, a thriving bead society, and internationally important bead businesses. This pattern is repeated in many parts of the world, lots of new beads are being produced, dying arts are being revived, and many old beads are being traded.

With this abundance of old and new beads in evidence, what can

you make with them? In *The Bead Book* we have tried to illustrate a wide

spectrum of the beads that are available and items that you can make

with them. The jewelry designs range from classic "pearl" chokers to

necklaces of brightly colored wooden beads used with rubber tubing.

Many of the necklaces have matching earrings, too. There are also ideas

uction

for presents, clothing, and items that can be used for interior decoration.

The aim is to inspire you – the projects can be copied exactly or adapted

for use with beads that you have already. Some of the beads used in the

book are easier to buy in the United States, and some are more readily

available in Europe, so make the most of what you can get and enjoy

being adaptable. We hope that the ideas in the book will inspire you and

that you will soon learn to add your own identity to them.

buying beads

In the introduction we have already mentioned some of the places where you can buy beads, but here we give more details of possible suppliers.

Firstly, there are bead shops. Most big towns have a specialist bead shop, or perhaps a craft supplies shop that sells a selection of beads. This, of course, is where you would have the greatest variety to choose from, and it is very nice to be able to actually see the colours and shapes before you commit yourself. It also gives you the opportunity to try looking at different beads together to see if they really will compliment each other. Some department stores now have a selection of beads in their haberdashery department; if you are keen on doing beadwork or embroidery with rocaille beads this is often a good source.

Secondly, you can buy by mail order, as there are now a host of useful catalogues available, mainly with good colour photography, which makes buying easy. The disadvantage of mail order is the frustration of waiting for your order to come when you have a project ready in your mind, and the acute frustration of items sometimes being out of stock when you have carefully chosen them. This having been said, the bead catalogues are invaluable if you live in a remote area, and they provide a wonderful selection.

What other sources are there? Antique markets will sometimes have damaged necklaces that are better re-made, and the charity shops often have strings of beads that you can re-use with other beads. Ethnic clothes shops usually have some beads that come from the countries that they are dealing with, and market stalls are another possible source. Do not forget to keep an eye out for beads when you are on holiday; although most countries export their beads to the United States and Europe, it is exciting to find them yourself. Finally, it seems that in some areas people are organizing bead parties in their homes, so it is a good idea to be aware of anything like that near you.

Beads are made out of many different materials: ceramics, glass, wood, plastic and bone, and more expensive materials including semi-precious stones such as malachite and lapis lazuli. The list is extensive, and in addition you should remember that there are materials that you can make beads from yourself; polymer clays, paper, air-dried clay and the like.

Most aspects of buying beads are a question of common sense, think of their condition; and check them for cracks or rough edges. Think carefully about the size of the holes in relation to the threads that you want to use: nowadays some beads like the Peruvian clay beads are made in the same designs with either large holes for leather or small holes for thread. Think about the types of beads that you are using together; it would be unwise to put very delicate beads between very heavy beads. Be aware of colour fastness: some brightly coloured wooden beads, for example, are susceptible to losing their colour. The content of metal beads needs consideration; some ethnic metal beads are either "white metal" or low-grade silver, whereas others can be very high-grade silver and can compare with sterling silver. If you are using semi-precious stone beads, or expensive glass beads, it is sensible to put high-grade silver with them, if possible. High-grade silver beads are likely to be priced by weight rather than per bead, although this is not a strict rule. There are also many beads available that are made from metallized plastic; these have a huge variety of good designs, and seem to be very durable.

Most beads are sized in millimetres (mm) with reference to their diameter (e.g. 6 mm spheres) or length times diameter (e.g. 15 x 4 mm tubes). The main exception to this is rocaille beads, which are the small glass beads, also known as seed beads, or sometimes pound beads, which

are used for bead weaving, bead embroidery and with beadlooms. These are sized by number – usually from 0/11 which are the smallest to 0/6 which are the largest. However, the sizing does vary according to the manufacturer, and can be reversed (i.e. 7/0); the basic guide is that the higher numbers are smaller sizes. Other beads often used in bead weaving, embroidery, etc. are bugles; these are small glass tubes, which come in sizes 4″ (or 4″), which are the largest, to 1″, which is the smallest (the size does not refer to inches!).

You will quickly learn the sorts of beads that you enjoy working with; some people only work with tiny beads, many others say that they do not have the patience to use small beads but will spend endless hours threading large dramatic beads. Do not forget, as you are hunting for your beads, that older beads represent a lot of history and are very collectible. In the same way, some of the beads that are being made now will be collectible in the future.

equipment and techniques

Round-nosed pliers

When you start to work with beads you can manage with very few tools. Scissors and pliers are the main necessity. Pliers are really a question of personal choice. If you are making a lot of straight ear-rings, then a small pair of *round-nosed pliers* is essential, and it is advisable to use pliers with short "noses" as long ones make your work seem remote. Again, if you are going to do a lot of work with wires, (eyepins, headpins or using jewellery wire), then a pair of *wirecutters* or snips will make the work easier.

Many of the necklaces in the projects are finished with french crimps or calottes, and you will need pliers to work with these. Once again it is a question of personal taste; *flat-nosed pliers* are often used but, as you will see from the step by step instructions, we have used *sprung round-nosed pliers* for this work. Some people find them more awkward, but they are often more powerful – because of this discrepancy the projects refer to necklace pliers, and leave the choice to you.

You will also need a selection of *needles*, very fine ones if you are working with tiny beads (the long thin beading needles are excellent for loom work), and blunter large-eyed needles will help with larger beads.

Wire cutters

If you are going to do wirework, then a *fine file* will be essential. Likewise if you do a lot of knotting or weaving, fine *tweezers* will be useful. This leads to the subject of *looms*. The most readily available beadlooms are metal, but they can be quite difficult to use and probably have put many people off this sort of beadwork. If you feel that you will have the patience to work with tiny beads, then it would be advisable to buy a wooden loom, which will make your work very much more enjoyable.

Flat-nosed pliers

Beading needles

It is useful to have some fast-acting *glue* to hand. This should never be allowed to dry beside good beads, as it will ruin them, but can be used in projects using inexpensive beads to decorative effect. It is also very effective for ensuring that knots stay tight.

You will need something to measure with, and having a mirror close to your work top is often helpful. Finally, do not forget that good lights are a most important part of your basic equipment.

Beadloom

threads

You have got your tools and your beads organized, and now it is time to consider what you will put them onto. The easiest threading material is *leather*, and a few beads with large holes, of course, put onto a thong, with some knots to finish it, can look stunning. The next material to consider is *nylon monofilament* (or fishing line, which is basically the same thing). This should be used with caution (some people say that it should never be used!), as it cannot be effectively knotted, so must be used with French crimps or calottes, and it produces stiff results, that do not hang very well. It also has a tendency to shrink, so if you use it, it is advisable to leave a small gap between your beads and fastener to allow for this. The advantage of nylon monofilament is that it has a rigid end for threading, will not fray, and is strong, so it is good for chokers or bracelets that do not need to hang well. It is also a good material for children to work with.

Tiger tail (or soft line) is another good strong threading material, made of wire with a plastic coating. It is excellent for use with heavy beads, but be careful when working with it, as it does not forget any kinks that are made in it, and can snap where it has been kinked. It is best to finish tiger tail with French crimps.

Nylon monofilament

Tiger tail

Actual threads are often made of polyester or similar manmade fibres. In this book we have mainly used a *thick polyester whipping twine* for heavy beads, or a *fine polyester thread* for small beads. Both of these are very strong and durable, and the thick one comes in several colours and can be supplied with a waxed finish, which makes it possible to use without a needle. This thread is ideal for knotting, plaiting and braiding, and can be used with calottes and French crimps. It hangs nicely and is ideal for most beads, as long as they do not have very small holes. However, if you use it with very heavy beads, it makes sense to allow your necklace to hang for a few days before you finish the ends, as the thread stretches to a certain extent. The thin polyester is also very strong and is excellent for weaving, loomwork or other use with small beads, and again it can be finished in many different ways.

Polyester thread

There are other synthetic threads on the market, all of which can be very useful. Another possibility is *silk thread*. This is mostly sold on cards, with an integral needle which is extremely helpful. Silk comes in lots of different colours and some different thicknesses, and again is extremely strong and hangs beautifully. The only drawback to it is that it is expensive.

As well as the threads that we have mentioned, do not forget that there are many beautiful *linen threads*, exciting cords and, of course, *chains* to be used. Once again, use your imagination, and, as you become confident with the techniques, you will be able to use all sorts of materials.

Silk thread

findings

These are the mysterious bits that hold everything together for you!

We will start with ear-rings. Straight ear-rings are threaded onto *eyepins* or *headpins*, both of which come in different lengths and in different finishes. Both are efficient, but eyepins have more versatility. To hang the ear-rings you need either *screw* or *clip fittings* for unpierced ears, or *earwires* for pierced ears. The most common earwires are *hook* (or *fishhook*) wires, *kidney wires* and *earstuds with hook*; the last type has a *butterfly* or *scroll* behind the ear. The names by which they are sold can

key

1 Hooks with jump rings	**15** Cones
2 Kidney wires	**16** Hooks with jump rings
3 Screw clasps	**17** Swivels
4 Hoops	**18** Eyepins
5 Screw/clip earwires	**19** Earwires (fish hook)
6 Triple spacer clasps	**20** Leather (or lace)
7 Earstud and butterfly	end crimps
8 Earstud with loop	**21** French crimps (gilt)
9 Headpins	**22** Hat pins with
10 Earwires (sterling silver)	safety ends
11 Trigger clasps	**23** Jump rings
12 Spring clasps	**24** Bolt rings
13 Earclips	**25** Figures-of-eight
14 Calottes	**26** French crimps
	(silver-plated)

vary slightly as you can see. Flat *earstuds* or *earclips* are what you need to make plain stud ear-rings. All the ear-ring findings that have been mentioned are available in silver plate, gilt plate, sterling silver and gold. Although for most people it is quite acceptable to use plated metals for the hanging parts of the ear-rings, it is advisable to buy the pure metals to go through the ears. Gold is expensive (but at least if you are making your own ear-rings you can re-use the findings), whereas sterling silver is usually very reasonably priced. However, some people can only tolerate gold, and, equally, some can only tolerate silver.

There are other findings that relate to ear-rings. For example, you can buy lots of different hangers that can add to the scope of your designs, and you can buy ready made hoops to which you can add beads.

For necklaces there is another range of findings. *Clasps* or *fasteners* come in many varieties with *bolt rings* (which are used with *jump rings*) perhaps the most conventional. There are also *screw clasps*, *torpedo clasps* and box clasps to name but a few. The box clasps often come with loops for two or three-strand necklaces, and plain *sprung box clasps* are very reliable as they seldom work undone. You can also buy beautiful fasteners that will be an integral part of your design (such as in the "triple pearl choker"). Do not forget that you can also buy attractive *hooks* and *rings*, or you can make them yourself. Most people will tolerate plated fasteners, but there are a few people who again have to wear pure metals.

Unless you use knots, you will need to attach your fasteners with *French crimps* or *calottes*, which come in different sizes. Leather or cord necklaces can be finished with *spring ends* or *leather crimps* (also called *lace end crimps*) and then a hook.

That covers the more basic findings for you, but if you go into a bead shop, or open a good catalogue, you will find a wealth of *spacer bars*, *cones* for multi-strand necklaces, *dropper hangers* for the ends of elaborate multi-strand necklaces, *bead caps* etc etc. As you grow more confident you will have the pleasure of trying them.

However, before we finish this section, there are a few other findings that should be mentioned including *figure-of-eight findings*, which are tiny pieces that change the way things hang, and *split rings*, which are more fiddly to use than jump rings, but are safer. You can buy long pins, with safety ends that are for *hatpins*, but you can clip them down if you are making long ear-rings with heavy beads. Do not forget about brooches. You could, for example, stick beautiful beads to *brooch backs*, or you might painstakingly thread small beads onto headpins and then into a *sieve finding* to create lovely brooches or earrings.

Not quite in the category of findings, but important to mention at this stage, is jewellery wire. This can be bought in different gauges, and in different finishes, i.e. silver-plated, brass etc. Getting used to using wire opens up new horizons in your work. In the book we have shown you how to wire "donuts" and to make your own hooks and jump rings. All good findings suppliers will also supply wire and it makes sense to explore the possibilities.

Silver wires

The great advantage of making jewellery with beads is that you can use fairly simple techniques in different situations and build your work. As we have illustrated in the book, once you have mastered the basic techniques you can use them in lots of different situations and produce very satisfying results. Starting with the basics – the first photograph shows you how to hold your pliers so that your control is good. To make a *loop*, hold your eyepin or headpin between your finger

wiring

and thumb, using the other fingers to control it as well. You need about 8 mm (⅜ in) of wire to make the loop. To make the headpin or eyepin the right length for the loop, either clip off any excess with wirecutters, or "fatigue" the wire by putting your pliers either side of it and gently moving the wire backwards and forwards until the metal breaks cleanly. Put your round-nosed pliers around the wire above your beads. Bring the wire towards you so that it is at an angle of 45 degrees from the straight piece, then move the pliers to the top of the wire and roll the wire away from you around the pliers. You do not have to do it in one movement. If you have not made a complete circle, take your pliers out and make the movement again, until you have a neat loop. If you then want to connect this loop into another one, for example to make a double-length ear-ring, open the loop sideways with your pliers, so that you do not damage the metal. The same applies to attaching an earwire; open the loop on the earwire sideways and add the loop on your eyepin or headpin.

You can, of course, do much more than just roll loops if you are using jewellery wire. It can be incorporated in your designs in many ways. Brass wire is rather springy and is harder to use, but silverplated wire is easier to manage, especially after some practice. Choose 0.8 wire for making decorative coils, or to wire a "donut" and 1.2 wire if you need something more rigid like a hook or a jump ring. It is hard to give precise measurements for wire work, as the items that you are planning to use will all vary. The wire is not expensive, so it is best to cut a piece of wire, keep a record of its length, and then practise and experiment.

To *wire a "donut"* or something similar, cut your wire in similar proportions to those shown in the photograph. Fold the wire through the "donut", leaving one end longer than the other. Roll the short end to make a loop. Then wrap the longer end around the bottom of the loop. Keep wrapping this wire until you have several neat coils, then clip the end, and gently press the top coil in with your pliers to make it neat.

To wire a "donut"

1

2

To make a jump ring

A *jump ring* can be made to match by rolling the wire round your pliers, or something else round, then clipping through the circles, and moving the ends together.

If you are threading beads onto wire and you want a more *elaborate and secure loop* at the top of them try the following. Bring your wire up, make a loop allowing extra wire, then wrap the extra wire under the loop. Again make several coils and press the end in neatly.

To make a *hook*, cut a few millimetres of wire, then file one end and turn a loop in this end. Now curve the wire back around your pliers, clip off any excess wire, bend up the end of this wire to make a good shape and file this end too.

To make a hook

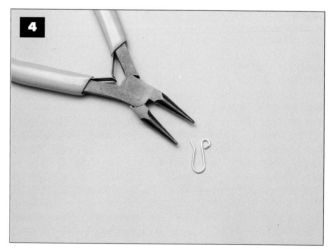

finishing

Leather or cotton thonging can be finished either with knots, or with *spring ends* or *lace end crimps*. Spring ends look like coils of wire, and you fit them to your thong and press the last coil into the leather with your pliers. The lace end crimps are folded around the thong from either side and squeezed with your pliers.

Spring clasps

Lace end crimps

The most simple way to finish a necklace or bracelet is by crimping the ends with French crimps. In the threads section we discussed which threads are suitable for crimping. To do this simply put one or two of the crimps onto the thread that you are using (in this case tiger tail), fold the thread through your fastener, and back through the crimps. Make sure that your crimps are close to your beads (except on fishing line which shrinks a little) and that your loop is neat but allows movement, and then squeeze the crimps firmly with your pliers. Make

French crimps

Calottes

sure that the crimps will not move on your thread, but do not squeeze so firmly that you damage the thread.

Another easy way to finish a necklace is to knot the thread (again we have discussed which threads are suitable), and then squeeze a *calotte* over the knot and attach your fastener to the calotte. You can put a drop of glue onto the knot before you cover it with the calotte, for extra safety, but make sure that the glue does not touch and spoil any precious beads. When you squeeze the calotte again make sure that you do not damage the thread.

Knots should be explained at this point. If you are finishing with a knot and calotte, or using a knot at the end of a tassel, and want to

To knot between beads

To make a double knot

make sure that the knot is close to your beads, put a needle into the knot before you tighten it, then draw the knot back towards the beads with the needle and gently pull the needle out when the knot is sitting next to the beads. *To knot between beads*, you need to allow approximately twice as much thread, as the length of your finished necklace. The length needed, of course, is dependent on the size of your beads and the number of knots, and you should allow even more thread if you are going to have a lot of knots, as it is easier to cut off the excess than to have to reknot due to lack of thread. Use a needle in the knots between beads in the same way as before, so that all your spacing is even. If your beads have larger holes you can make double knots to go between them.

Knots are another appropriate way of finishing a necklace and *attaching a fastener*. To do this make a single knot next to your beads, and leave a needle in it. Put on your fastener, leaving space for more knots between it and the knot with the needle in it. Then put the knots into

Attaching a fastener

this space, remembering how many you have used, and how much space you left, so that you can duplicate on the other side. When you have made these knots, put your thread into the needle that you left in the knot, and pull the needle through to tighten everything. Either put a drop of glue onto the last knot and cut off your loose thread, or if you have large enough holes, thread back into your beads.

If you have a few special beads, another way to finish them is to braid the ends. The technique that we have used is a simple macrame technique. You need three strands, either single or double. When your strands are ready, leave the middle one in place and work the left-hand

Finishing a multi-strand necklace

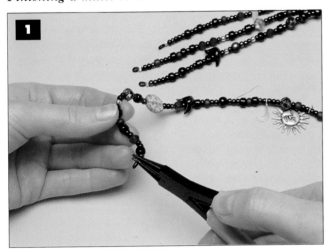

hand strand under the middle and over the right-hand strand. Work the right-hand strand over the middle and under the left-hand strand. Continue in this way as the braid builds. You can knot the ends or add a fastener, and braid back over the ends that attach the fastener.

Braiding is one good way to finish a multi-strand necklace. Another way to do this is to make loops with crimps at each of the ends, and then pass another thread with a loop at the end through these loops and back into itself. Put a bell cap or a cone over all the ends, and either thread more beads onto the single string, or finish on the single string. You can also loop all the single crimped ends onto wire and into a bell cap or cone.

Braiding the ends

beadwork

The other techniques that we have not discussed are the actual beadwork techniques. Beadwork is usually done with rocailles or bugles, or other small beads, and takes the form of either free-hand weaving, such as the Peyote stitch that we have used on the hat band, or loomwork, such as that used for the evening bag.

Free-hand weaving does not have to be done with tiny beads, as we have shown in the Inca choker. To work your beads together as in the example here, use two threads and two needles, and put the threads in from either side of the long beads, so that they cross in the middle, bring the needles back out of the beads, thread a bead or several beads between them, and then thread into the next bead from either side. Keep working in this way. You can also make *fringing* for necklaces, or to go on scarves, by working your threaded needle down through your beads, adding a

Free-hand weaving

Fringing

small bead at the bottom, and then working back up your other beads. They will hang down and the small bead will hold them in place.

To work in *Peyote stitch*, thread on a few beads (we have used three here), then holding the bottom thread, add another bead and work back into the first bead using the same colour and pull your thread through. Then pick up another bead in the same colour as the second bead and work back into the second bead, and continue in this way, tightening the thread and making a rope of beads.

Peyote stitch

There are many other designs that you can make using free-hand weaving; we have only illustrated the ones that are used in the book.

Loomwork is another area that is covered only in its simple forms in the book, though we hope to inspire you to want to learn more. To thread a loom, cut your threads about 25 cm (10 in) longer [at each end] than your work will be and cut one more thread than you will have beads. These are the warp threads. Knot them together and place the knot over the pin on the far end of your loom. Wind them around once or twice so that they are held securely. Now bring the threads back

towards you, separating them into the grooves on the loom (it is helpful to use a needle to do this). Tie the loose ends onto this end of the loom, so that they are very taut. If you are making a long piece of work, wind the lengths of warp threads around the roller at the far end, so that it is firmly held, before you tighten your wing nuts, and knot on the loose ends at your end. To work the beads on the loom, attach your thread to one side, and work a few rows by putting this thread in and out of the warp threads. Then put the beads that you need onto your needle, holding them beneath the warp threads. Bring the beads up between the threads and pull the thread through, then bring your needle back into the same beads, this time making sure that the beading thread goes above the warp threads. Pull the needle tight at the end of each row so that the beads are held firmly. You will continue to work in this way as you add the pattern to your design. It is sensible to work out the design that you are going to use on graph paper before you start. Before you take your work off the loom, work a few rows with just the thread, as you did at the beginning. Work all your loose ends, and your warp threads back into your strip of beading.

Loomwork

classic

designs

~

triple pearl choker
and ear-rings

YOU WILL NEED:

For the necklace:
91 x 10 mm pearls
100 x 0/7 black rocailles
6 french crimps
6 x 3 mm silver-plated
balls
140 cm (4ft 8in) tiger tail
clasp

For the ear-rings:
2 pearl cabochon
1 pair studs + butterflies

TOOLS ETC:

necklace pliers
glue

T his necklace is simple to make but looks very sophisticated. It is worth buying a really beautiful clasp for it to set off the pearl beads and make the most of them.

1 Thread the pearl beads onto 3 graduating lengths of the tiger tail, with a black rocaille between each bead. We have 28 pearl beads on the top row, 30 on the middle row and 33 on the bottom row.

2 Finish each row with a rocaille, a silver-plated ball and another rocaille, and then crimp to the fastener and trim the ends of the tiger tail.

3 For the ear-rings, simply glue a stud to the back of the cabochon.

black "jet"
choker

These faceted glass beads have been designed to look like jet beads, so we have designed a choker that could have come from a Jane Austin novel with them. It is made with simple free-hand weaving.

1 & **2** Cut 2 x 150 cm (5 ft) of thread; this is a generous amount, but will save the risk of running out of thread. Use two needles with it. Knot the ends of the threads together. Put a rocaille, a 5 mm bead and a 6 mm bead onto each

thread, then thread into another 6 mm bead from either side so that the threads cross inside the bead. Add another 6 mm bead onto each thread and then again work from either side into the next bead. This is the basic weaving for the choker.

3 After five central beads, put a rocaille, a 6 mm bead and another rocaille onto your bottom thread. Thread back up through the 6 mm bead and the top rocaille, leaving the bottom one to hold the hanging beads.

4 Continue to weave, adding more hanging beads, and starting to use the larger (8 mm) beads. Return to the smaller beads towards the other end of the choker, so that both ends match.

5 At the end of the choker make sure that the threads are pulled securely through, so that there are no gaps in the weaving, then knot the ends together. Put a calotte over the knots at both ends.

6 Cut a small piece of chain for each end and open a link in the chain to attach it to the calotte. Add your hook to one side (this can be put into the chain at different lengths so that you can wear the choker in different ways).

knotted Chinese necklace
and ear-rings

These lovely Chinese porcelain beads have been combined with little enamelled bead caps to highlight their colours. We have used a thick thread and knotted between the beads, so that you can learn how to knot while you make a beautiful necklace.

1 Knot your thread and put a calotte over the knot.

2 Thread the first bead with the bead caps either side of it and make a knot after the bead (the knot is shown in the techniques section).

3 Continue to add the beads and bead caps and the knot between each bead. Finish with a knot after the last bead. Put another calotte on the knot.

4 Attach the fastener to your calottes.

5 The ear-rings are simply threaded onto the eyepins with a rolled top.

pearl chain
and ear-rings

For the chain:
ready-made pearl chain
with **80** beads
10 x 8 mm pearl beads
4 x 6 mm pearl beads
4 x pearl oval beads
14 x 6 mm metallized
plastic rose beads
8 x 3 mm silver-plated
balls
10 x 50 mm eyepins
2 x 25 mm eyepins

For the ear-rings:
20 x 8 mm pearl beads
32 x 3 mm silver-plated
balls
8 x 0/7 white rocailles
5 cm (2 in) chain
18 x 25 mm (1 in) headpins
2 x 38 mm (1½ in) eyepins
1 pair earwires

round-nosed pliers
wirecutters

T*his is a simple way to use readymade pearl chain with an effective result. We have added very dramatic ear-rings to go with the simplicity of the chain.*

1 Cut the pearl chain into eight lengths, each of which has 10 of the little pearls on it. Thread the patterns for the straight pieces onto your 50 mm eyepins and roll the tops. We have made four the same and two with different patterns.

2 Gently open the loops on the eyepins to hook in the pieces of chain.

4 For the ear-rings, start by making the pieces on the headpins which have a silver-plated ball on the end, a pearl and then either a white rocaille, or another silver-plated ball. Roll the tops of the headpins.

5 Cut two 2.5 cm (1 in) pieces of chain and hook the headpin pieces into them.

3 For the middle and the back of the chain make linked pearl pieces. Two longer straight pieces are linked onto a short (25 mm) eyepin which has one pearl on it.

6 Hang the chains from the bottom of the eyepins, put more pearl beads and silver-plated balls onto them, clip the ends and roll their tops. Attach the earwires to the top of these eyepins.

looped loom
choker

T his choker is dark and sophisticated, but is an easy start to using a beadloom.

1 Cut nine 80 cm (2 ft 7 in) lengths of the thin polyester thread and position them onto the loom. Both outside edges should have two threads in one groove of the loom to give a firmer edge. Attach another long thin thread to one of the outside warp threads, and work this in and out of alternate warp threads to give a neat beginning to the looming.

2 Start to work the beads onto the loom. Pick up six beads with your needle and hold them beneath the warp threads making sure that they fit neatly between each one. Pull the needle and thread through the beads, still holding the beads in place with your finger.

YOU WILL NEED:

1 g 0/8 purple rocailles
110 x 0/7 grey rocailles
3 x 5 mm purple glass
beads
thin black polyester
thread
thick black polyester
thread

TOOLS ETC:

beadloom
fine beading needle
scissors
masking tape
(optional)

4 Cut two pieces of the thick thread 60 cm (2 ft) long for each end of the choker.

5 Plait on the new threads, using them together, and all the warp threads together. It helps to tape the choker to your work surface so that you can make the plaiting firm and close to the end of the looming.

3 Thread your needle back through the same row of beads, making sure that your needle is above each of the warp threads. Continue with your looming, changing to grey beads initially after 10 rows and then after every five rows. Roll the beadwork back towards you as you work along the loom, keeping the work tightly together. You will need to make the choker about 23 cm (9 in) long. Finish with a few rows of thread only as at the beginning, and remove the choker from the loom.

6 When your plaiting is long enough to tie the choker round your neck, knot all the ends together, and trim them neatly.

7 If you have loose ends from joining new threads work these back into the choker with your needle.

8 Now start on your loop design. Cut a new piece of thin thread and work it through a few rows of work before the third stripe in the choker. Now thread down the stripe, thread on 12 more rocailles, alternating grey and purple, and bring the needle up five rows along, before the next stripe. Work back down this stripe and thread on eight more rocailles in alternate colours and then a purple glass bead. Add one more grey rocaille as "stopper" and thread back up through the glass bead and the rocailles.

9 Work one more loop using 15 rocailles, and then make one using 19 rocailles, both with alternating colours. Your needle should now be threading up through the sixth stripe in your choker. Bring the needle neatly BACK along the top of three rows of looming, working in and out of the outside loom thread, and then thread down the middle row of rocailles. Thread another hanging piece to go into the middle of the loop using 4 rocailles and another purple glass bead, held with another rocaille. Work back up this to the bottom of the choker, and take the thread back along the bottom of the choker to start to form another of the loops. You can then complete the loop pattern to match the first half, and weave the end of the thread through a few extra rows of rocailles to secure the loops. Finish by trimming any loose ends.

tiffany style necklace
and ear-rings

For the necklace:
1 oval porcelain bead
4 tube shape porcelain beads
8 x 8 mm pink glass beads
8 x 6 mm clear glass beads
4 large clear glass drops
2 small clear glass drops
20 g (¼ oz) 0/9 clear rocailles
3 m (10 ft) white polyester thread

For the ear-rings:
2 oval porcelain beads
6 clear rocailles
2 x 8 mm pink beads
2 x 50 mm (2 in) eyepins
1 pair earwires

scissors
needle
glue
round-nosed pliers for the ear-rings

*P*ale and delicate with lovely porcelain beads and shimmering glass. The necklace is made to wear long, with an exciting cluster of beads at waist length. There are simple ear-rings to compliment it.

1 Cut 2.5 m (c 8 ft) of thread and use it double with a needle. Knot the ends and put glue onto the knot. When the glue is dry, thread the first beads and drops and rocailles onto the thread and then the large oval bead.

2 Thread on, working the round beads, tubes and drops into the rocailles and making a long plain area for the back of the necklace. Keep working back down the necklace, whilst checking that the two sides are matching. Now thread back into the round bead, rocaille and oval porcelain bead near the beginning of the necklace. Put on the last few beads and knot at the end. Put a drop of glue onto the knot.

3 Cut another 50 cm (1 ft 8 in) length of thread, and use it double with a needle again. Knot and glue the end and thread a few more of the hanging beads. Carefully knot this thread under the oval bead and above the hanging pieces.

4 Thread on the last few beads and knot the end of this thread. Trim off the loose ends.

5 The earrings are simply made by putting the beads onto the eyepins with a rolled top.

evening
bag

YOU WILL NEED:

90 g (3 oz) 0/7 iridescent
blue rocailles
20 g (¾ oz) 0/7 iridescent
clear rocailles
10 g (⅜ oz) 0/7 light blue
rocailles
a piece of black felt **10 x
20 cm (4 x 8 in)**
1.5 m (5 ft) black cord

TOOLS ETC:

*beadloom
beading needle
scissors
glue
needle*

*T*his project will require time and patience, but your effort will be
rewarded. The bag is made in strips on a beadloom, then lined with felt
and finished with cords. It is big enough to carry your keys and some money for
a glamorous night out.

1 Set up the beadloom as shown in the
techniques section. There are 11 rocailles
in each strip. You will need three strips
and there are 57 rows in each strip.
Remember to introduce the colour
changes differently on the central strip.

2 When the three strips are complete,
work the loose threads at the sides of the
strips back into the weaving. Then
connect the strips together by running a
thread through all of the pieces.

3 Knot the warp threads together and
trim them.

4 Glue the piece of felt to the beading, making sure that all the loose ends of threads are trapped between the two.

5 Sew neatly along all the edges so that the felt and the beading cannot separate.

6 Fold the piece in half and sew the cord down the sides, making sure that you have the bottom of the cord neatly tucked under.

amber necklace
and earrings

For the necklace:
9 oval amber beads
10 round amber beads
6 amber tube beads
10 Indian silver beads
2 bead caps
2 silver discs
1 silver fastener
1 silver split ring
silk thread

For the ear-rings:
2 x 50 mm (2 in) eyepins
2 round amber beads
2 amber tube beads
2 Indian silver beads
4 silver discs
1 pair earwires

needle
round-nosed pliers for
the ear-rings
scissors

*B*eautiful chunks of Baltic amber are threaded with plain chunky silver beads and ornate bead caps as a centre piece. The amber is so lovely that it does not need to have much added to it.

1 Join the silk thread to the fastener with knots (as shown in the techniques section). Five knots were used here.

2 Thread the beads onto the silk, using the bead caps on the central bead.

3 Join the split ring to the necklace using five knots as before.

4 The ear-rings are simply put onto the eyepins and the tops are rolled. The earwires are put into the top loop on the eyepins.

ethnic

designs

pipe
choker

T his is a nice easy way to use pipe beads and create a dramatic effect with them. The pipe beads are actually plastic but they look very natural. We have put them together with some elaborate spacer bars and a pretty ceramic ring to create a piece that is light and easy to wear.

1 Cut 6 x 60 cm (2 ft) lengths of the waxed thread, and thread 16 rocailles onto each one. Thread three onto each side of the ceramic ring, and arrange the rocailles so that they are evenly positioned on the threads inside the ring.

2 Now thread both ends of each thread through a pipe bead, so that you have three on each side, add the rocailles and work the double thread into a spacer bar.

3 Work on into the second spacer bar and more pipe beads, and then work all the threads into a single pipe bead. Repeat on the other side of the ring. Move all the beads back up the threads so that there are no gaps.

4 Cut two 140 cm (4 ft 7 in) lengths of the brown cord and tie one around each bunch of waxed threads. When you have tied the cords to the threads, add a drop of glue so that they will not slide down the waxed threads.

5 Braid each cord around the waxed threads, as shown in the techniques section. You may find it easier to tape the choker to your work top while you braid. Knot the ends of your braiding threads at the bottom of the waxed threads and leave trailing pieces of the brown cord.

cinnabar
cluster

*A*pple coral and cinnabar beads, in three strong strands held by a dramatic centrepiece.

YOU WILL NEED:

65 brown tile beads
230 x 0/7 black rocailles
80 x 5 mm black beads
40 tiny sandalwood beads
19 x 10 mm apple coral beads
2 x 14 mm apple coral beads
10 nut beads
8 oval cinnabar beads
4 black and red cinnabar beads
1 very ornate cinnabar bead

2 cones
10 cm (4 in) 0.8 silver-plated wire
fastener
french crimps
black polyester thread

TOOLS ETC:

round-nosed pliers/necklace pliers
scissors
all-purpose glue
needle
wirecutters

1 Cut three lengths of thread about 60 cm (2 ft) long, lay them out, and start to plan your design. You will be using nearly all of the beads on the main strands. Keep 3 x 10 mm apple coral beads, 15 x 5 mm black beads, 19 brown tile beads, 3 sandalwood beads and 40 black rocailles to make the centrepiece with the large cinnabar bead, and the ends of the necklace. In this design you will need to keep the centre of the strands quite plain, use smaller beads at the ends of the strands, and space your larger beads evenly through the design. Your strands should be very slightly different lengths, and should hang well together.

2 Finish each end of the strands by making a neat loop with french crimps. Trim off any loose ends of thread. Cut the wire into two pieces and make a generous loop at one end of the pieces. This is opened sideways so that the ends of the necklace strands can be hung from it, and then closed again. Thread a cone onto each of the wires so that the ends of the strands are neatly covered. Add a few more beads to these wires at each side. Then roll the wires and use this loop to attach your fastener.

3 Make the centrepiece by cutting a 30 cm (1 ft) piece of thread and knotting one end. Put a drop of glue onto the knot and allow it to dry. Thread up into the large cinnabar bead, put on more of the smaller beads, and then thread back into the large bead.

4 Finish with the last few beads and make another knot in your thread. Use a needle to draw the knot close to the bottom of the beads, and put a little glue onto this end. Trim the thread close to the knots. You can now loop the centrepiece round the middle of the necklace strands.

peruvian
string

*S*imple but stylish – with a few tricks to make your necklace look really professional.

14 assorted glazed
Peruvian beads
6 plainer ceramic tubes
blue linen thread

measuring block
glue
needle
scissors

1 Cut a 180 cm (c 6ft) length of the blue linen thread and position a bead in the middle of it. Make a knot either side of the bead and use a needle to move the knots close to the central bead. Use a measuring block to make the spaces between your beads. (Ours is 5 cm or roughly 2 in long). Position the block next to the knot that you have just made and use a needle to move another knot into position at the end of the block.

2 You can now thread another bead, and knot close to the other side of this bead. Continue with your beads, knots and spaces, working on both sides of the string, moving away from your central bead.

3 Thread both ends of the string through either side of your last bead.

4 Use your measuring block to check the distance between this bead and the ones on either side of it, and make a knot on both sides of the last bead. Put a drop of glue onto these knots and trim the ends of the string very neatly.

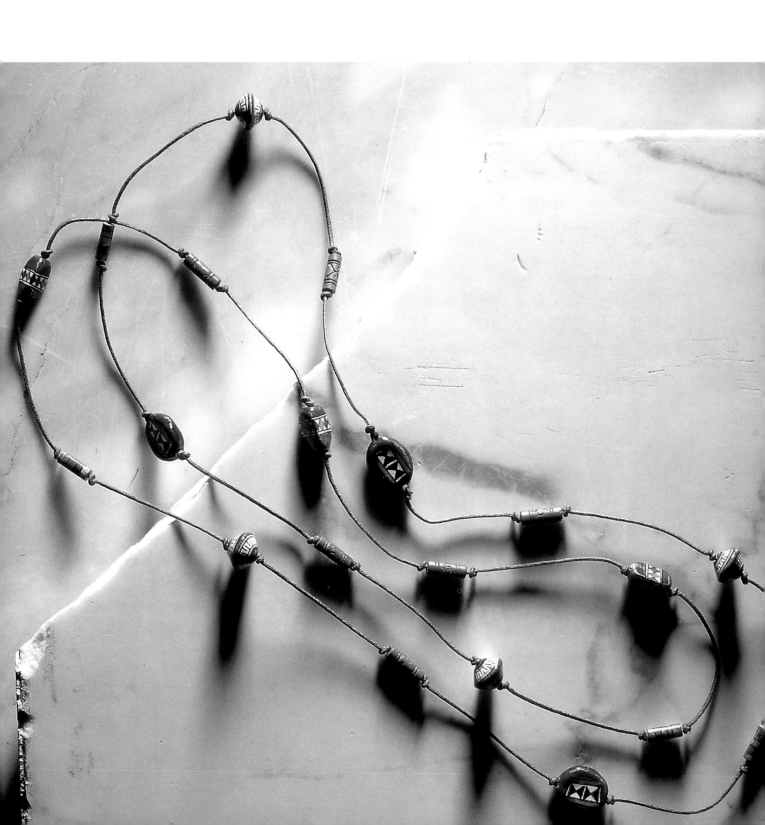

lapis lazuli and

turquoise necklace

1 x 90 cm (3 ft) string of
Chinese turquoise chips
1 large lapis lazuli bead
4 x 8 mm lapis lazuli beads
4 coral chunks
14 x 7 mm Thai silver
beads
3 cards of no. 5 black silk
thread
2 calottes
Balinese hook fastener +
jump ring

TOOLS ETC:

necklace pliers
scissors
fishing line to plan
the necklace on

T his necklace is a wonderful combination of chips of Chinese turquoise,
large lapis lazuli beads from Afghanistan, old coral from Nepal, and tiny
silver beads from Thailand. It is completed with a Balinese clasp. A necklace
for dreaming of faraway travels!

1 & **2** The chips of turquoise cannot be
counted to get even lengths, and the odd
sizes need to be balanced around the
necklace, so it makes sense with this

necklace to plan it on fishing line. You
can also reject any damaged chips or
ones that sit badly at this stage.

3 Unwind the silk thread on your cards
and knot the ends together. Put some glue
onto the knot and then put a calotte over
the knot. Rethread your necklace onto the
silk, working each section back towards
the calotte as you thread.

4 Finish with another knot and calotte as
before. Attach the hook and the jump ring
to the calottes.

Indian braided
beads

*T*his is an effective way to use a few special beads, and makes an
interesting change from putting them on leather. Use really bright threads
that pick up the colours of the beads and make them look bright and beautiful.

1 Cut 5 m (16½ ft) of each colour
thread, which you will use double. Then
cut two 1 m (3¼ ft) lengths of two of the
colours, which will go through the middle
of the beads, as the core threads. Thread
one of the beads onto the middle of these
two pieces.

2 Knot the braiding threads onto the
core threads. Start to braid over the core
threads, as shown in the techniques
section. You may find tape useful to hold
the braid in place.

3 When you have made 11 cm (4½ in)
of braiding, put a bead onto the core
threads. You may need to double the
piece of tiger tail around the core threads
to work them through the bead.

4 Bring your braiding threads round the sides of the bead, and start to braid again on the other side.

5 Braid the threads 10 times between the beads. Continue to add the other eight beads.

6 When you have added all the beads, braid on for another 9 cm (3½ in), and knot the threads together. Using the core threads and the braiding threads, make two tiny plaits, just long enough to go over a bead. Then knot all the threads together again, and trim the ends, so that they are all the same length.

Inca choker
and ear-rings

*S*mall ceramic tube beads have been woven together on either side of a metallized plastic "Inca" disc. Then it is tied around the neck so that you can wear it as tight as you like. It will not take long to make, and you might find yourself wearing it every day. We have used black beads, but you could let your imagination run riot and even have a spectrum of colours around your neck.

1 Unwind the silk on the cards, and knot the threads together about 18 cm (7 in) from the end. Thread on the first few beads and balls.

2 Thread into the first tube from either side, so that the threads cross inside it.

3 Add another 4 mm bead onto each of the threads before you thread into the next tube. Continue to weave in and out of the tubes until you have eight tubes on this side.

4 Thread the central beads and balls onto each thread and then bring both of them through the Inca disc.

5 Repeat the weaving through the tubes on the other side of the Inca disc. Tighten the beads and tubes on the threads and then knot them together. Cut a 2 m (6½ ft) length of thick black thread for each end, fold each in half, and attach them to the ends of the choker, by the knots. Slip a 5 mm black bead on at each end, and braid the ends below these beads. Knot the end of the braiding and trim the ends.

Thread the ear-rings onto the eyepins with a rolled top.

native American
belt

A very bright, cheerful representation of a Native American beaded belt. The one that we show here has patterns that we have designed, rather than authentic ones. If you wanted to make your belt more special, you could check original colours and designs in a library, and make yourself a more true representation.

1 Thread your loom as shown in the techniques section, and start to work on your rocailles. There are 11 rocailles across the belt.

2 Follow the pattern, or design your own pattern and complete that. This beaded strip is 64 cm (2 ft 1 in) long. When you have taken it off the loom, work all the loose threads back into the work. Tie your warp threads together so that they can be hidden away.

3 Cut the two pieces of chamois. We have cut them from a piece from a motorist's shop. Sew the two strips together, and cut a small patch to go over the join.

4 Glue the beading to the chamois, making sure that the knotted warp threads are carefully tucked beneath the beading and the leather. Then sew the beading to the chamois for extra strength. Fringe the ends of the chamois.

5 Finally, thread on the beads and knot the fringes beneath the beads.

African beads
on leather

a pendant
6 Venetian millefiore
beads
6 Venetian eye beads
26 Ghanaian powder
glass beads
40 old silver rings
18 mm bead with a wide
hole
5 x 5 mm black glass
beads
2 spring ends for leather
1 m (3¼ ft) natural
leather thonging

wirecutters
pliers

*T*hese are old Venetian glass beads that were sent to West Africa, and old powder glass beads from Ghana. The pendant piece is made by the Lobi people and shows a coin and snakes; the snakes are considered to have protective powers.

1 Arrange your beads onto your leather with a silver ring between each one.

2 Work both ends of the leather through the wide holed bead. Make sure that it is a strong bead.

3 Clip the loops off the spring ends and squeeze them onto the ends of the leather with the other small black beads behind them.

Thai silver necklace
and ear-rings

For the necklace:
13 large silver beads
14 medium silver beads
6 small ribbed silver beads
34 small plain silver beads
4 tiny silver beads
1 trigger catch
1 jump ring
grey silk thread

For the ear-rings:
2 large silver beads
2 medium silver beads
2 small plain silver beads
2 tiny silver beads
2 x 50 mm (2 in) eyepins
1 pair earwires

TOOLS ETC:

scissors
needle
round-nosed pliers

A simple but stunning arrangement of silver beads from Thailand. The beads are made using the traditional skills of the Khymer craftsmen, who have come over the borders from Cambodia.

1 Start by knotting your thread onto the fastener (as shown in the techniques section); there are four knots between the first bead and the fastener.

2 Thread your beads. As these beads are handmade they are slightly different shapes and sizes, and you should arrange them so they sit well together.

3 Finish by knotting on to the jump ring at the other side of the necklace.

4 The ear-rings are simple straight ear-rings with rolled tops.

glitz

designs

~

triangles necklace
and ear-rings

For the necklace:
72 x 8 mm blue faceted beads
107 x 0/7 grey rocailles
8 x blue triangle beads
2 calottes
1 fastener
3 m (10 ft) black polyester thread

For the ear-rings:
4 blue triangle beads
6 x 0/7 grey rocailles
2 x 8 mm blue faceted beads
4 x 38 mm (1½ in) eyepins
1 pair earwires

necklace pliers
round-nosed pliers for the ear-rings
2 fine needles

A striking combination of iridescent beads and angular shapes all worked together to produce a necklace that will allow you to make an entrance – anywhere.

1 Cut two 150 cm (5 ft) lengths of thread and use them double with the fine needles. Knot the ends and put a calotte over the knot. Thread a rocaille onto both pairs of threads, separate the threads into the first faceted beads with rocailles either side of them. Bring all the threads into the next bead, working from both sides so that the threads cross in the centre of the bead.

2 Continue to weave through the first section of beads, then bring both threads through a triangle bead. Now use triangles and weaving, changing the direction of the triangle beads as you work.

3 Bring both threads through the hanging beads, put a rocaille onto the bottom and thread back up through the beads above it, so that the rocaille holds the beads on the hanging piece.

4 Repeat your design on the other side of the choker. When you have finished check that the beads are neatly positioned on the threads, then knot again at this side and put another calotte over the knot. Add the fastener.

5 The loop on the top of the bottom eyepin on the ear-rings is linked into the bottom of the top eyepin, so that the ear-ring has extra movement.

baubles and
bangle set

For the necklace:

21 x 12 mm (2 in) metallized plastic balls
35 x 6 mm frosted lamp beads
64 x 5 mm black glass beads
132 x 0/6 red rocailles
58 x 3 mm turquoise balls
3 glass roses
12 french crimps
1 bar and circle fastener tiger tail or thread

For the bracelet:
80 x 0/6 red rocailles
48 x 3 mm turquoise balls
4 x metallized plastic roses
40 x 5 mm black glass beads
16 x frosted lamp beads
2 x 2-hole spacer bars
2 x 3-hole spacer bars
4 circles of sprung bracelet wire
8 safety ends

For the ear-rings:
2 ornate clips
6 x 50 mm (2 in) eyepins
8 x 0/7 black rocailles
6 x frosted lamp beads
2 glass roses
12 x 0/6 red rocailles
4 x metallized plastic roses

necklace pliers
round-nosed pliers
scissors
wirecutters
glue

T*his set is a lovely mixture of bright colours and dull silver-coloured beads. We started our design with the clips for the ear-rings and added the glass rose beads to compliment the fruit and flowers pattern on them. Next came the smart bracelet, again with little roses, and finally a simple twist necklace with the last few glass roses entwined in it.*

1 For the necklace cut three 45 cm (1½ ft) lengths of tiger tail and attach them to one end of the fastener with crimps. Thread the beads and crimp again at the other end. The necklace can be worn plain or twisted.

2 To make the ear-rings, thread the beads onto the eyepins, clip them to length, and roll the tops to attach them to the clips.

4 Now thread beads onto the top two wires and add a three-hole spacer to these new wires. Join in the top wire from the first pair. Work on round on all of the wires, putting the same pattern into the centre.

3 The bracelet is the most complicated piece to make. Cut the lengths of wire and glue four safety ends to each of them. Thread the first few beads onto the bottom two wires and thread on a two-hole spacer bar.

5 Reverse the pattern round to the other side adding the other spacer bars. Then glue the safety ends to the other side to keep all the beads in place.

rope
necklace

40 g (1½ oz) 0/7 white
rocailles

20 g (¾ oz) each of 0/7
turquoise, light blue and
dark grey rocailles

1 metallized plastic bead

5 m (16½ ft) fine white
polyester thread

1.25 m (4 ft) white waxed
thread

ring clasp

fine needle
scissors
glue

This is a very easy necklace to make. Lots of rocaille beads are threaded into long strings, and looped together. You could wear them just like that, clasped so that the strings are twisted together. Or you can add a tassel to make them more exciting.

1 Cut the fine thread into 1 m (3¼ ft) lengths and make two strings of white rocailles, and one each of turquoise, light blue and dark grey. The strings of rocailles should measure 90 cm (c 3 ft) long which allows you length to knot the threads. Put a drop of glue onto the knot and trim the ends.

2 These can now be held together with the clasp. Twist them before you wear them.

3 Cut five 20 cm (8 in) lengths of the waxed thread for the tassel. Knot the ends of the threads and put a drop of glue onto the knots. When this is dry, thread on the rocailles, again two strands of white and one each of the other colours. Leave enough space to knot the other end of the thread. Do not knot too close to the rocailles, as you do not want the tassel to be rigid. Put another drop of glue onto these knots and trim all ends.

4 Put your last piece of waxed thread into the middle of these strands and thread into the metallized plastic bead.

5 Thread in pattern onto the other side of the large bead, 14 rocailles on one side, 15 on the other. Knot the two ends of thread firmly together, again put on a drop of glue, and trim the ends. This can just slide over your necklace twist. Matching ear-rings can be made with shorter tassels, and using an eyepin to come up through the big bead.

Greek tubes and bars
necklace and ear-rings

For the necklace:
2 x 3-hole spacer bars
40 Greek ceramic tubes
51 x 0/7 metallic purple
rocailles
fastener
french crimps
hatpin or stiff wire
tiger tail

For the ear-rings:
2 ceramic tubes
4 small ceramic square
beads
2 x 6 mm metallized
plastic balls
10 x 0/7 purple rocailles
2 x 50 mm (2 in) eyepins
1 pair earwires

strong round-nosed
pliers
necklace pliers
wirecutters
file

T*his necklace is glamorous and stylish – the strength of the beads compliment the strong shape of the design.*

1 Cut either a stiff wire or a hatpin wire to a 12 cm (5 in) length and smooth the ends with a file. Roll one end with your pliers and thread on the rocailles and the tubes and the spacer bars. Then roll the top of the wire.

2 Cut two 74 cm (2½ ft) lengths of tiger tail. Fold one in half and put a rocaille into the middle of the length. Now using the tiger tail double, thread more tubes and rocailles and work through one side of the spacer bars.

3 Repeat this on the other side of the spacers with the other length of tiger tail and work up both sides of the necklace, alternating tubes and rocailles.

4 Push all the beads back down the tiger tail and make neat loops at the ends with french crimps. Hook the fastener into these loops.

5 Use the 50 mm (2 in) eyepins to make matching ear-rings. These are simple drop ear-rings.

pink glitz necklace
and ear-rings

For the necklace:
26 x 8 mm pink beads
52 x 6 mm pink beads
2 antiqued gold triangles
1 antiqued gold ring
140 cm (c 4 ft 8 in) black thread
10 gilt french crimps
22 x 3 mm gold-plated balls
180 x 0/6 red rocailles
1 ornate fastener

For the ear-rings:
6 x 38 mm (1½ in) eyepins
22 x 0/6 red rocailles
14 x 3 mm gold-plated balls
8 x 8 mm pink beads
6 x 6 mm pink beads
2 x antiqued gold triangles
1 pair earwires

round-nosed pliers for the ear-rings
necklace pliers
scissors

*A*s the name suggests, this is another really glitzy necklace. Both the rocailles and the round beads have a extra sheen and depth to their colour to add to the richness of the piece.

1 Cut three pieces of the thread, increasing in length between 30 and 35 cm (1 ft and 1 ft 2 in). Thread the ring into the middle of them and then arrange the pink beads and rocailles onto each of the threads.

2 When you have finished the arrangement, crimp the ends of the threads onto the triangles, putting a rocaille between the crimp and the triangle.

3 Cut two 15 cm (6 in) lengths of thread and crimp these to the tops of the triangles in the same arrangement as before, then thread the beads onto these threads. Attach the fastener with crimps, again putting a rocaille between the fastener and the crimps at each end.

4 Make the hanging pieces for the ear-rings by threading the eyepins and rolling their tops. Then open these loops sideways to hang the pieces from the triangles. Put the earwire into the top of the triangle.

red hearts necklace
and ear-rings

For the necklace:
5 metallized plastic
hearts
4 red lacquered hearts
12 x 8 mm red hearts
20 x 8 mm a.b. hearts
24 x 5 mm red hearts
12 x 6 mm round a.b
beads
27 x 5 mm black glass
beads
130 x 0/7 black rocailles
34 x 0/7 red rocailles
2 french crimps
56 x 25 mm (1 in) eyepins
50 cm (c 1 ft 8 in) red
thread

For the ear-rings:
2 metallized plastic
hearts
2 x 8 mm a.b. hearts
8 x 0/7 black rocailles
4 x 0/7 red rocailles
2 x 50 mm (2 in) eyepins
1 pair earwires

necklace pliers
round-nosed pliers
scissors
wirecutters

T his necklace is really glitzy. Lots of different-sized hearts, in different colours, are all threaded together into a Valentine's riot.

1 Start by making the little eyepin pieces for the necklace, simply threading the beads and rolling the tops of the eyepins. There are: 20 x large a.b. heart + black rocaille; 12 x large red heart + black, red, black rocailles; 16 x small red heart + black, red rocailles; 4 x small red heart + black, red, black rocailles; 2 x small red heart + black rocaille. The eyepins should be clipped to the appropriate length before you roll them, as shown in the techniques section.

2 Start to thread your necklace from the centre. Put on one rocaille and then thread both ends into a heart, a rocaille and a 5 mm black bead before you separate the threads and add the red lacquered hearts.

3 Thread the eyepin pieces on with the beads in small clusters, there are nine in each of the first two clusters, and five in the second two. Between them thread the large hearts and the black glass beads, with black rocailles beside them.

4 When you have threaded the main part of the necklace, work to the end with the plainer beads, and crimp on the fastener.

5 The ear-rings are simply threaded onto the eyepins with a rolled top.

gilt chain
and ear-rings

This chain is very simple to make. We have seen a very similar one on sale in a store in Los Angeles for nearly $100; think of that as you make your own!

For the chain:

70 cm (2 ft 4 in) chain

10 x 50 mm (2 in) eyepins

34 x 3 mm gold-plated balls

14 x 0/8 purple rocailles

8 x 0/8 green rocailles

6 x 5 mm crystal lice-shaped beads

8 x 4 mm crystal diamonds

4 x 6 mm metallized plastic gold-plated roses

10 x 8 mm metallized plastic gold-plated roses

1 crystal drop

20 x gold-plated daisy lice

1 x 6 mm jump ring

For the ear-rings:

8 x 38 mm (1½ in) eyepins

4 x 25 mm (1 in) eyepins

10 cm (c 4 in) chain

10 x 5 mm crystal diamonds

40 x 3 mm gold-plated balls

6 x 0/8 purple rocailles

2 x 6 mm jump rings

1 pair earwires

round-nosed pliers
wirecutters

1 Make your straight pieces, threading the beads onto the eyepins and rolling the tops as shown in the techniques section.

2 Cut eight pieces of chain that are 5 cm (2 in) long, and one piece that is 30 cm (1 ft). Gently open the loops at the top and bottom of your eyepins, sideways, and slip in the lengths of chain, to make up the pattern.

3 Finish with a straight piece at each end, and join these with a jump ring through their loops and through the crystal drop.

4 For the ear-rings, make the hanging pieces on the eyepins first, clipping them to length where necessary. Thread these onto the last 38 mm (1½ in) eyepins, and roll the ends of these, making sure that the new loops face in the same direction as the ready-made loops.

5 Gently open the loops sideways, and add the pieces of chain (four 2.5 cm (1 in) lengths). At the top of the ear-rings use the jump rings to join the chain, and to attach the earwires.

night sky
necklace

M ulti-strands of stars, moons and birds, and a dramatic haematite donut, all hanging from tiny dark iridescent rocailles.

YOU WILL NEED:

1 haematite donut
(20 mm (¾ in))

1 sun

6 round mosque beads

12 cube mosque beads

10 mother-of-pearl birds

84 x 5 or 6 mm glass beads
in black, purple and
blues

2 tiny heart beads

6 black ceramic birds

15 iridescent miracle
beads (6 – 8 mm)

6 stars

2 moons

a few 3 mm silver-plated
balls

c 350 x 0/7 dark
iridescent rocailles

2 cones

fastener

tiger tail

french crimps

0.8 silver wire

9 figure-8 fittings

black polyester thread

TOOLS ETC:

necklace pliers
wirecutters
scissors
round-nosed pliers

1 Cut a 6 cm (2½ in) piece of wire, put it through the donut and cross the ends over. Form one end into a neat loop with your pliers. Use your fingers to wrap the other wire around the bottom of this loop. When you have covered the bottom of the loop with a few neat coils, clip off any extra wire and press the end of the wire into the loop above the coils with your pliers. The figure-8 fittings are used to hang the sun, and the tiny stars and moons.

2 Cut four 50 cm (1 ft 8 in) lengths of thread and start to thread on your beads. The donut and the sun should be in the same position on the threads. Space all the bigger beads and the hanging pieces in the more central part of the strands, and work towards plainer, smaller beads at the sides. You need to keep a selection of beads to go either side of the cones. When you feel that your threading is right, hold the strands up to see how they hang. If you want them all to hang together, the strand with the donut should be the shortest.

3 Finish all of the ends by making neat loops with the french crimps, then trim any loose ends. Cut a 12 cm (*c* 5 in) length of tiger tail for each end and make a loop at one end with crimps. Thread the tiger tail through the ends of the necklace strands and back into its own loop. Thread a cone over the ends of the necklace strands.

4 Your last few beads are then threaded onto the tiger tail, and you can attach the fastener at the ends with more french crimps. Finally trim any loose ends.

f u n

designs

~

modern art choker
and ear-rings

For the choker:

1 wooden square bead
1 blue circle bead
1 pink triangle bead
1 pink small square bead
1 mauve small square bead
2 small blue cubes
2 green cubes
2 yellow lice beads
2 red washer beads
2 pink round beads
4 x 0/7 black rocailles
45 cm (1½ ft) round black tubing
1 packet of 0.8 jewellery wire
4 cm (1½ in) 1.2 jewellery wire

For the ear-rings:
2 mauve small square beads
2 pink triangle beads
2 red washer beads
2 yellow lice beads
2 large green cubes
2 small blue cubes
2 pink round beads
8 x 0/7 black rocailles
2 x 50 mm (2 in) eyepins
2 x 25 mm (1 in) eyepins
1 pair earwires

round-nosed pliers
wirecutters
flat-nosed pliers

N ot all projects with beads need to have lots of threading. With this necklace we have wired most of the beads so that they hang flat, and threaded a few, to create a bright, primary choker.

1 Start by wiring the beads that are going to hang flat, as shown in the techniques section. Check that the loop you make is large enough for the rubber tubing to go through, before you make the coils at the bottom of it. Cut about 8 cm (3 in) of wire for each bead.

2 Cut another two pieces of wire the same length, make a neat loop at the bottom, and thread on the beads, to make the hanging pieces. Make a large loop above the beads so that it will go over the rubber tubing and coil your wire below it.

3 Use the end of the rubber tubing to make the spirals that go round it.

4 Thread the design onto the tubing and gently press the ends of the spirals into the rubber so that the pattern remains separated. You can gently press in the loops above the beads as well, so that they stay in place.

5 Make another loop at the end of the rubber tubing, turn the wire at an angle to it, and wind the wire round the loose end. Attach a hook to this and hook it into the other side to fasten the choker.

Make the ear-rings by linking the two eyepins together when you have threaded the beads.

glass fantasy necklace
and ear-rings

For the necklace:
9 assorted glass nuggets
37 blue drops
51 blue and green
teardrops
52 x 6 mm blue and green
round glass beads
18 x 0/8 rocailles in green
or blue
60 x 3 mm silver-plated
balls
2 cones
4 x 38 mm (1½ in) eyepins
10 crimps
170 cm (5 ft 7 in) blue
thread
1 packet 0.8 silver-plated
wire

For the ear-rings:
2 matching nuggets
1 pair earstuds +
butterflies

round-nosed pliers
necklace pliers
wirecutters
glue for ear-rings

T*his is a lovely, over-the-top combination of beads, wire and glass nuggets. The nuggets are usually sold for display or flower arranging, but they combine beautifully with the rich blues and greens of the beads to make a really exotic necklace.*

1 Start by working the wire round your glass nuggets. Cut a 25 cm (10 in) length of wire and make a coil at the beginning of it. Press a glass bauble into the coil so that it starts to enclose it.

2 Continue to wrap the wire around the nugget until it is held firmly in place.

3 Make a loop above the nugget and coil the wire around the bottom of the loop, as shown in the techniques section. Trim off any excess wire. Wire the other nuggets in the same way.

4 Put four of the glass drops onto eyepins, roll the top to hang with the beads. Now plan out the design for the necklace on your threads. Cut three 40 cm (1 ft 4 in) lengths of thread, and work your beads, nuggets and drops onto the threads. Arrange them so that the colours and shapes are well balanced, and finish each of the threads with the rocailles which will go inside the cones.

5 When you are happy with these threads crimp a neat loop at their ends. Cut two 15 cm (6 in) lengths of threads and make a loop with crimps at one end. Thread these through the loops at the ends of the main threads, and back into themselves. Then put your cones over the ends.

6 Thread the rest of the beads above the cones and finish by crimping on the fastener.

7 The studs are glued onto the back of the two nuggets to make matching ear-rings.

chain
belt

12 ceramic disc beads
1 packet 1.2 silver-plated wire
60 cm (2 ft) large link silver-coloured chain (from a DIY shop)
6 cm (2½ in) 0/8 silver-plated wire (optional)

strong round-nosed pliers
an extra pair of strong pliers
wirecutters
file

An idea for something different that you can make with beads. These large discs are from Rajastan and have lovely soft colours, but they are a little heavy for necklaces or ear-rings. So this is a design for a belt.

1 Cut lengths of wire to go through your discs (you will need about 6 cm (2½ in) for each bead). Make a large loop at each side of 11 of the beads. The 12th bead has one large and one small loop.

2 Open the chain in three-link lengths (you may need to use two pairs of pliers to do this), and link the chain and the beads together, ending with the 12th bead with the small loop at the very end.

3 Add two extra links of chain before the first bead. Make a hook with 6 cm (2½ in) of the thicker wire as shown in the techniques section. As an extra decoration you can wrap the thin wire around the hook, if you like.

flowers and leaves necklace
and ear-rings

YOU WILL NEED:

8 tiny plastic flowers
8 larger flowers
8 smaller leaves
5 larger leaves
4 white glass drop beads
13 figure 8 findings
16 x 25 mm (1 in) silver-plated headpins
38 x 6 mm clear beads
76 x 0/7 pearl rocailles
16 x 0/7 clear rocailles
30 x 6 mm clear glass beads
8 x 8 mm pink glass beads
tiger tail
4 french crimps
fastener

TOOLS ETC:

round-nosed pliers
necklace pliers
scissors

T*his is a delicate, pretty necklace with pastel leaves and flowers, which is very light and easy to wear in the summer.*

1 Put the leaves onto the figure 8 findings.

2 Put the headpins into the flowers (with a rocaille inside them) and make a loop on top of them.

3 & **4** Arrange your flowers, leaves and

beads onto the tiger tail and crimp the fastener on at either end.

102

"donuts" necklace
and ear-rings

For the necklace:
8 ceramic donuts
2 spacer beads
27 grey cube beads
42 blue round beads
4 long grey beads
56 x 4 mm purple beads
2 cones
180 cm (c 6 ft) thread
1 packet 0.8 wire

For the ear-rings:
2 donuts
2 blue round beads
2 grey cube beads
6 x 4 mm purple beads
0.8 wire
2 x 38 mm (1½ in) eyepins
1 pair earwires

TOOLS ETC:

round-nosed pliers
necklace pliers
scissors

These ceramic beads from Greece come in soft, mottled colours You could just wire one of the "donuts" and wear it on a thong, or you can make something really extrovert like the necklace shown here.

1 Wire the "donuts", as shown in the techniques section. Then cut three 60 cm (2 ft) lengths of thread and plan the beads and donuts onto the threads, so that they hang well together.

2 Take your threads through the spacer beads when you are happy with the design.

3 Bring all your threads through the beads on the side pieces.

4 Crimp the end of each of the threads, making a small loop. Then cut a short piece of wire, make a loop on its end and hook the ends of the threads into this loop. Put the cones over the wire and turn another loop to attach the fastener.

5 The ear-rings are made by wiring the "donuts" and attaching an eyepin to the wire for the top beads.

fish chains
and ear-rings

For the chains:

10 fish beads

14 fish-shaped beads

24 x 50 mm (2 in) eyepins

28 x 22 mm (1 in) silver-plated swivels

2 cm (¾ in) 1.2 silver-plated wire

59 x 3 mm silver-plated balls

28 cm (11 in) silver-plated chain

31 x 0/7 grey rocailles

For the ear-rings:

6 fish-shaped beads

6 x 50 mm (2 in) eyepins

22 x 3 mm silver-plated balls

12 x 0/7 grey rocailles

6 x 12 mm silver-plated swivels

2 x 7 mm jump rings

1 pair earwires

round-nosed pliers
wirecutters

T*his is a very cheerful piece of jewellery, with lots of blue ceramic fish and fish-patterned beads swimming around your neck. They are even linked with swivels that are actually made as fishing tackle, and then silver-plated for jewellery use.*

1 Make up the straight pieces with your fish beads and fish-shaped beads on the eyepins. Arrange the silver-plated balls and rocailles around these beads.

2 Link the pieces together with the swivels by gently opening the loops on the eyepins sideways.

3 Lay the four lengths of chain and beads together to make sure that the lengths and arrangements are right. Make a large jump ring, as shown in the techniques section, for each end and connect the necklace together.

4 Add a piece of chain to each end, and make a hook for one of the ends. This is shown in the techniques section.

The ear-ring beads are put onto eyepins and then hung from the smaller swivels, and put onto jump rings and the earwires.

charm
bracelet

*T*his is a very jolly collection of brass chain and brass and copper beads.
We have made a really musical charm bracelet with fish and elephants.

1 Make the hanging pieces for the bracelet using the beads, balls and the fish and elephant beads, clipping off any excess length on the eyepins and turning loops at the top.

2 Open the loops sideways to hang these pieces from the chain.

3 Put the fastener onto the chain with the jump rings.

rainbow collar
and ear-rings

For the necklace:

17 x 36 mm (1½ in) rainbow drops

14 x 20 mm (¾ in) rainbow drops

26 x 5 mm round beads

62 x 0/7 black rocailles

27 x 50 mm (2 in) eyepins

40 cm (1 ft 4 in) silk thread

2 calottes

11 cm (4¼ in) chain

1 readymade hook or 1.2 wire

For the ear-rings:

2 x 38 mm (1½ in) rainbow drops

2 x 5 mm round beads

4 x 0/7 black rocailles

2 x 50 mm (2 in) eyepins

1 pair earwires

round-nosed pliers

wirecutters

scissors

glue

*I*t was suggested that this could also be called a Rasta necklace because of the predominance of colours. This is a very easy necklace to make, and it would never go unnoticed!

1 Put your drop beads onto the eyepins, clip off any extra length, and make loops at the top of them. Four of the smaller drops have rocailles, or round beads and rocailles, above them.

2 Make a knot at one end of the thread, and put a drop of glue onto the knot, then put a calotte over the knot. Thread your beads and the beads on eyepins onto the thread.

3 Again knot the silk at the end and put another calotte over the knot. Trim the loose ends of thread.

4 Add a piece of chain on one side of the necklace, and a hook to the other side, so that you can wear the collar at different lengths.

The ear-rings are simply put onto the eyepins with rolled ends.

accessories

and gifts

~

decorated
box

S*imple decorations make a plain box look opulent and exciting.*

1 Mark the design onto the box lid

2 Use paper glue to stick the beads onto the box. Start with the ridged sides. Put glue into some of the grooves and then put two bugles and a gold rocaille into each one.

3 Stick on the central glass cabochon. Then start glueing beads along the straight lines on your box lid. Use your needle to position the bugles with a gold rocaille between each one.

4 Spread more glue into the centre of each triangular section. Position a few more bugles in these sections. Sprinkle the gold rocailles liberally onto the rest of the glue. Now work on the other sections of the box. When you have finished the design, check the positioning of all the beads and leave the box to dry.

embroidered
blouse

Yet again, we let the design on the item suggest the project to us! You could draw a design onto a garment and then embroider the beads onto that, as we have shown on our sample piece. Or you can choose something like the blouse illustrated, which already had a design on it, and was enormous fun to embroider.

1 You could sew on individual beads using a backstitch. Or you can work small sections by threading a few beads onto your pattern, and then bring your thread back through from the other side and catch your beaded thread, to stop the beads having too much movement.

If you were doing a very beautiful piece of bead embroidery, you could use couching. To do this you have your beads on one thread, and use another thread to come from below between each bead to secure them.

Don't forget to only use beads that can be washed if you are embroidering with them.

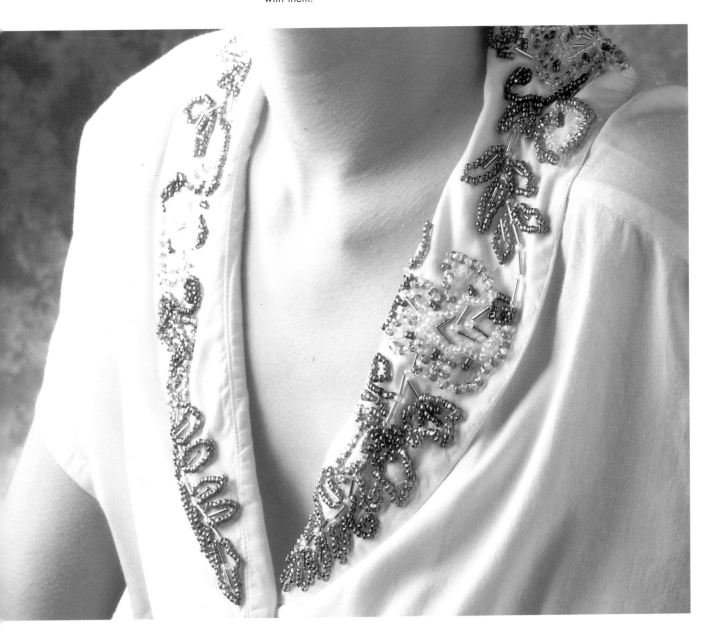

bead

curtain

Y ou can use beads to great effect as a window decoration. It is sensible to choose reasonably inexpensive beads as even a small curtain will require a lot of beads. The effect is very rewarding. We give dimensions and numbers of beads for the curtain illustrated, but if you want a different-sized curtain you will obviously need to adjust these.

40 cm (1 ft 4 in) angled
doweling
29 x 135 cm (c 4 ft 6 in)
polyester thread
284 silver bugles
79 dark blue bugles
145 turquoise bugles
81 green bugles
28 x 5 mm faceted beads –
light blue
32 x 5 mm faceted beads –
green
34 x 5 mm faceted beads –
dark blue
14 x 6 mm faceted beads –
light blue
c 600 x 0/7 rocailles
c 60 french crimps

TOOLS ETC:

*wood stain, or
permanent marker
fine needle
scissors
necklace pliers
bradawl*

1 Cut the piece of wood to length and make sure that it does not have rough ends. Then stain it. We used a permanent marker, so you could stain to a colour to match the beads, or your room.

2 Work out how many strings of beads you are going to hang and measure along the top of your wood. Then make holes through the wood with a bradawl.

3 Thread one rocaille into the middle of your pieces of thread, to hold the beads at the bottom, then thread double through the other beads.

4 Bring the threads up through the wood and put two crimps onto the top of the threads to hold them in place. The crimps will be hidden by the angled wood. Hang the curtain from right-angled hooks.

spider's web
hat

a hat
rocailles
bugles
10 mm round flat beads
small hearts
thread

needle
scissors

The hat was already interesting, but the design of it seemed to ask to have beads added and, of course, they ended up like spider's web. The strings of beads have been left loose on the hat, so that the movement becomes part of the design. The sample piece is shown flat for clarity and shows how you could add the stripes in beads too on a plain hat. We have not given precise amounts for the beads, as every hat (and head!) is different.

1 & **2** The sections of beads are strung onto the thread and then a small stitch is made to attach that section to the hat. If your hat has a lining, open a small section, so that you can work from both sides. You can then restitch it later.

hat
band

about 20 g (¾ oz) each of three colours of the 3 mm beads
1 x 10 mm bead for the rosette
polyester thread

fine needle
scissors
glue

I f you do not want to have beads all over your hat, another good idea is to make a hat band with beads. We have used glass beads with a lovely sheen to them, with a Peyote stitch to weave them together. This does require patience, but the band looks stunning.

1 Cut a 150 cm (5 ft) length of thread, knot the end and work it double through the large bead. Thread on one each of red, green and blue beads in sequence, repeat four times, and pick up the knotted end of the thread to hold the beads in place.

2 Work on from here, threading red into red etc for five rows, making a rosette round the large bead. Leave the end of the thread in place.

3 Thread red, green and blue beads onto a new long thread and then thread back into them with the same colour so that you make a spiral of beads. Keep working in this way until you have created the right length for your hat, with the rosette between the two ends. The spiral of beads will be quite stretchy, so make sure it does not get too long. When you knot on a new thread it is a good idea to put a drop of glue onto the knots as the polyester is very slippery. Always try to avoid getting glue onto the beads.

4 Use the thread at the end of the spiral to weave through the rosette to join them, then use the loose thread from the rosette to work into the beginning of the spiral to join the circle completely.

curtain
tie-backs

YOU WILL NEED:

polyester thread
an assortment of beads

TOOLS ETC:

strong needles
scissors

When we saw these tie-backs, we felt that they needed some beads! Again the ones that we show here should only be considered inspirational, as you will find different tie-backs, and your colour schemes will be different.

1 For the top of this tie-back use rocailles to "anchor" the big rust beads, making them rather like exotic fruits.

2 Beneath the rust beads are natural wooden beads, with a rocaille on either side of them. Think here of your positioning so that the beads are evenly spaced.

3 The final section has black glass beads sewn into the little loops on the tie-backs.

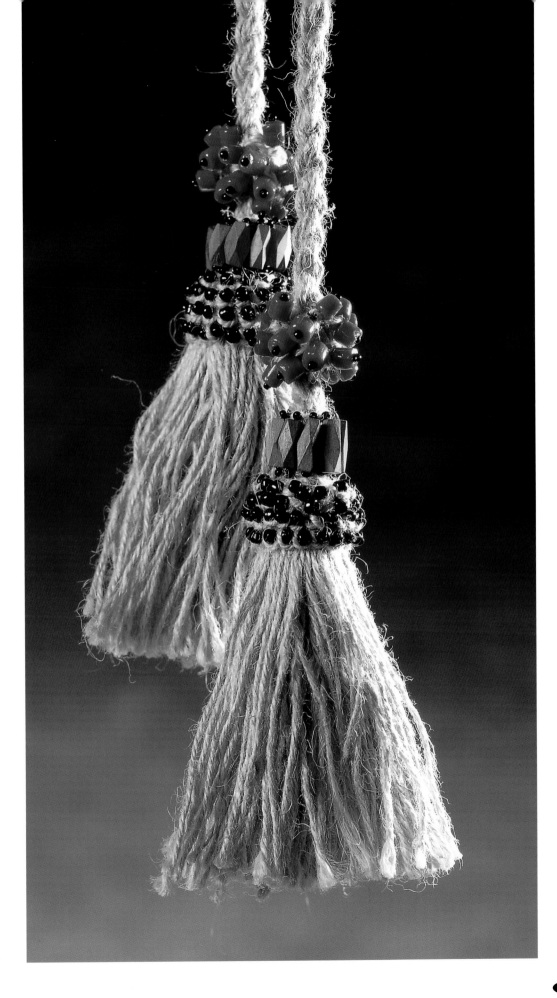

frame

YOU WILL NEED:

1 frame
100 x 4 mm purple beads
100 x 0/7 grey rocailles
40 x 0/8 green rocailles
15 x turquoise bugles
fine black polyester
thread

TOOLS ETC:

strong glue
needle (to move
beads)

*T*his is an easy way to make more of a plain frame. The colours of the beads gave the idea for the bunch of grapes design, but the scope is enormous, and you could really let yourself go with ideas for decoration.

1 You could either make your design on paper first, or just arrange the beads onto the frame and then move them off a piece at a time to add the glue.

2 The bugles are best threaded onto short pieces of thread to glue them into place. When the glue is dry, you can remove the pieces of thread.

ACKNOWLEDGEMENTS AND SUPPLIERS The Publishers are grateful to the following suppliers for their help and cooperation.

BEAD SHOP
43 Neal Street
Covent Garden
London WC2H 9PJ, UK

HOBBY HORSE LIMITED
15–17 Langton Street
London SW10 0JL, UK

LONDON BEAD COMPANY
25 Chalk Farm Road
London NW1 8AG, UK

BEADS (retail only)
259 Portobello Road
London W11 1LR, UK

CREATIVE BEADCRAFT LIMITED
Denmark Works
Beamond End
Nr Amersham,
Bucks HP7 0RX, UK

JANET COLES BEADS LIMITED
1 Shire Business Park
Wainwright Road
Worcester WR4 9WS, UK

BEAD SOCIETY OF GREAT BRITAIN
Carole Morris
1 Casburn Lane
Burwell
Cambs CB5 0ED

BEADWORKS
139 Washington Street
Norwalk,
CT 06854, USA

PERUVIAN BEAD COMPANY
1601 Callens Road
Ventura
CA 93003, USA

CREATIVE BEAD IMPORTS
255 South Terrace
South Fremantle
Western Australia

MAIL ORDER ONLY
(send a stamped addressed
envelope)

BOJANGLES
Old Cottage
Appleton,
Oxon OX13 5JH, UK

AHENZI
91 High Street
Winslow
Bucks MK18 3DG, UK

WORKSHOPS WITH
SARA WITHERS

Available through
OXFORD ARTS & CRAFTS
Gable end
Hatford
Near Faringdon,
OXON SN7 8JF, UK